Scott Foresman

Math Around the Clock

SUMMER SCHOOL • AFTER SCHOOL • INTERSESSION

Algebra: Integers and Graphing

PEARSON

Scott Foresman

Editorial Offices:
Glenview, Illinois • Parsippany, New Jersey • New York, New York

Sales Offices:
Parsippany, New Jersey • Duluth, Georgia • Glenview, Illinois
Coppell, Texas • Ontario, California • Mesa, Arizona

MW01275632

ISBN: 0-328-06372-X

2 3 4 5 6 7 8 9 10 V004 12 11 10 09 08 07 06 05 04 03

Math Around the Clock

Contents

Unit 7 • Algebra: Integers and Graphing

Complete the number square. All rows, columns, and diagonals have the same sum.

1,032	952	a
b	1,000	1,016
984	c	968

Name _____

Example

In the table at the right, the same rule is used with each number in Column A and the corresponding result is given in Column B. Write the rule using words and using a variable. Let the variable represent any number in Column A.

The rule is: Multiply by 7. If n represents any number in Column A, the rule could be stated $n \times 7$.

A	B
1	7
2	14
4	28
5	35
7	49
9	63

Find the rule for each table. Give the rule using words and using a variable. Let the variable represent any number in Column A.

1

A	B
2	8
3	9
14	20
21	27

_____

_____

2

A	B
24	12
20	10
16	8
14	7

_____

_____

3

A	B
27	24
20	17
18	15
12	9

_____

_____

4

A	B
2	8
4	16
5	20
7	28

_____

_____

5

A	B
10	1
14	5
22	13
26	17

_____

_____

6

A	B
12	2
18	3
24	4
30	5

_____

_____

7

A	B
7	15
10	18
11	19
15	23

_____

_____

8

A	B
50	10
40	8
35	7
25	5

_____

_____

Variables and Tables (continued)

Find the missing values in each table. Find the rule for each table. Give the rule using words and using a variable. Let the variable represent any number in Column A.

 9

A	B
0	0
8	2
12	
20	5
28	
40	10

_____

_____

10

A	B
7	5
9	
15	
16	14
20	18
25	23

_____

_____

11

A	B
0	0
1	9
4	
5	45
7	63
10	

_____

_____

12

A	B
3	
5	22
7	24
12	29
25	
32	49

_____

_____

Write each rule using a variable.

 13 Multiply a number by 2.

_____

14 Add 12 to a number.

_____

15 Divide a number by 3.

_____

Write each rule using words.

16 $n + 3$

_____

_____

17 $n \times 8$

_____

_____

18 $n \div 17$

_____

_____

19 $n \times 21$

_____

_____

20 What rule could be used to find the number of feet in n yards? Write the rule using words and using a variable.

_____

21 **Test Prep** Choose the correct letter for the answer.

Find the rule for the table at the right.

A $n + 8$ **B** $n \times 5$ **C** $n \div 5$ **D** $n + 12$

A	B
$n = 0$	0
$n = 3$	15
$n = 5$	25
$n = 7$	35

Name _____

Variables and Tables

1 Find the rule for this table.

A	B
30	20
40	30
50	40
60	50
70	60

A Add 10.

B Subtract 10.

C Multiply by 10.

D Divide by 10.

3 Find the rule for this table.

A	B
13	1
26	2
39	3
52	4
78	6

A Subtract 12.

B Multiply by 13.

C Divide by 13.

D Add 12.

2 Find the rule for this table.

A	B
5	20
10	40
12	48
15	60
20	80

F Multiply by 4.

G Add 4.

H Divide by 4.

J Subtract 4.

4 What rule could be used to find the number of months in n years?

F $n \times 12$

G $n \div 12$

H $n + 12$

J $n - 12$

Oral Directions Choose the correct letter for each answer.

Write the ordered pair for each point.

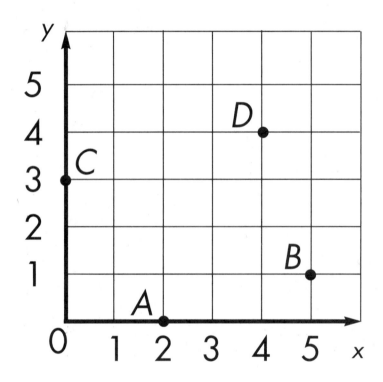

Name _____

Coordinate Graphing

Example

Use the grid at the right to write the ordered pair for each point.

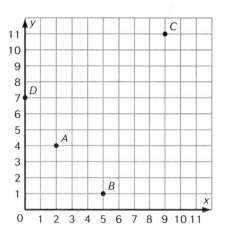

A
Start at 0.
Count to the right 2 spaces.
Count up to Point A 4 spaces.
The ordered pair for A is (2, 4).
C
The ordered pair for C is (9, 11).
D
The ordered pair for D is (0, 7).

Use the grid at the right for Exercises 1–10.
Write the ordered pair for each point.

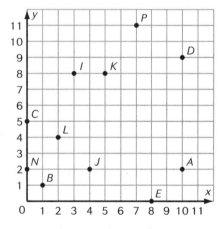

1 A **2** C **3** I

4 P **5** N **6** L

7 B **8** E **9** K

10 D

On grid paper, graph and label the point located by each ordered pair.

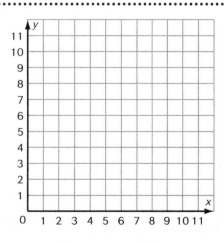

11 A (2, 2) **12** B (4, 2)

13 D (6, 6) **14** E (10, 0)

15 G (7, 8) **16** H (10, 4)

17 J (0, 1) **18** K (0, 10)

19 C (7, 1) **20** F (1, 3)

Name _____

Coordinate Graphing (continued)

Use the grid at the right for Exercises 21–32.
Write the ordered pair for each point.

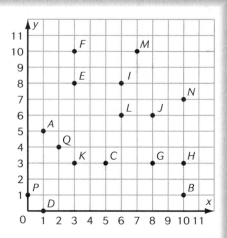

 21 E _____   **22** N _____

 23 A _____   **24** K _____

 25 P _____   **26** B _____

Name the point located by each ordered pair.

27 (5, 3) ___   **28** (10, 3) ___   **29** (2, 4) ___

30 (6, 6) ___   **31** (3, 10) ___   **32** (8, 6) ___

Use the grid at the right for Exercises 33–35.
Each unit represents one city block.

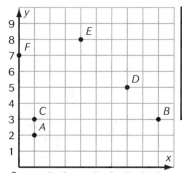

Key
A Post Office
B Grocery Store
C Bank
D Bakery
E Gas Station
F School

 33 Name the building located at (1, 3).

_____

34 Write the ordered pair for the
location of the school.

_____

35 **Math Reasoning** Katherine rode her bike from the grocery
store to the bank. How far did she ride?

_____

36 **Test Prep** Choose the correct letter
for the answer. Use the grid at the right.

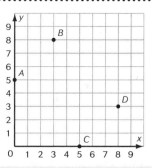

Find the ordered pair for Point C.

A (0, 5)   **B** (1, 5)   **C** (5, 0)   **D** (5, 1)

Name _____

Coordinate Graphing

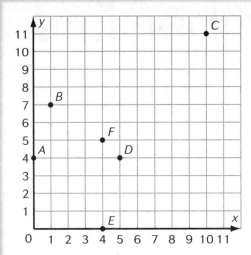

Use the grid above for Exercises 1–5.

1 Find the ordered pair for Point *C*.

   A (10, 10)

   B (11, 10)

   C (11, 11)

   D (10, 11)

2 Find the ordered pair for Point *E*.

   F (0, 4)

   G (4, 0)

   H (4, 4)

   J (3, 4)

3 Name the point located by the ordered pair (0, 4).

   A *D*

   B *E*

   C *B*

   D *A*

4 Name the point located by the ordered pair (5, 4).

   F *D*

   G *E*

   H *B*

   J *C*

5 If the coordinates at (*x, y*) are (4, 7), what are the coordinates at (*x* + 2, *y* + 2)?

   A (2, 5)

   B (9, 6)

   C (6, 9)

   D (5, 2)

Oral Directions Choose the correct letter for each answer.

Copy the number line and label the missing numbers. Name the coordinate for each point.

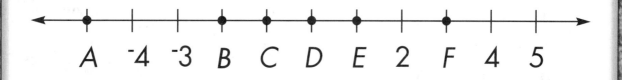

A   ⁻4   ⁻3   B   C   D   E   2   F   4   5

Name _____

Meaning of Integers

Example

Write an integer for each word description.

a. A temperature of 5 degrees below zero

$^{-}$**5**

b. A gain of 20 yards

$^{+}$**20**

c. 6 steps backward

$^{-}$**6**

d. 100 feet above sea level

$^{+}$**100**

Write an integer for each word description.

1 a withdrawal of $50

_____

2 a loss of 30 yards

_____

3 500 feet below sea level

_____

4 15 degrees above zero

_____

5 9 steps forward

_____

6 a deposit of $25

_____

7 12 degrees below zero

_____

8 400 feet above sea level

_____

© Scott Foresman

Name _____

Meaning of Integers (continued)

Write an integer for each word description.

9 4 steps backward

_____

10 A gain of 13 yards

_____

Use the number line for Exercises 11–14. What is the coordinate of each point?

11 A _____

12 B _____

13 C _____

14 D _____

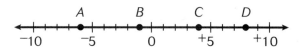

For Exercises 15–17, place each integer on the number line.

15 ⁻7   **16** ⁻2   **17** 3

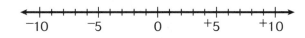

18 A man started walking at an elevation of 0 feet above sea level. He walked up 50 feet and then down 12 feet. What was his final elevation?   _____

19 **Test Prep** Choose the correct letter for each answer.

Which word description identifies an integer of ⁻5?

A A deposit of $5   **C** A gain of 5 yards

B 5 degrees above zero   **D** 5 steps back

20 A man walked 3 steps backward and then 4 steps forward. Which integer identifies his final location?

F ⁺1   **G** ⁻4   **H** ⁻3   **J** ⁻1

Name _____

Meaning of Integers

1 Which word description identifies an integer of ⁺100?

  A An increase of 50.

  B A decrease of 100.

  C An increase of 100.

  D No change.

2 Margaret made a deposit of $50 in her savings account. A few days later she made a withdrawal of $20. Which integer identifies the balance in her account?

  F $20

  G $30

  H $40

  J $70

3 The temperature at 8:00 A.M. was 0 degrees. By 10:00 A.M. it had risen 5 degrees. Which integer identifies the temperature at 10:00 A.M.?

  A ⁺5°

  B ⁻5°

  C 0°

  D ⁺10°

Use the number line below to answer Exercises 4–6.

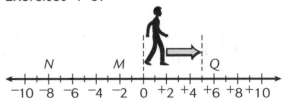

4 What is the coordinate of the Point Q?

  F ⁻6

  G ⁺6

  H ⁻4

  J ⁺4

5 Which of these coordinates is to the left of Point N?

  A ⁻1

  B ⁻5

  C ⁻9

  D 0

6 Which of these coordinates is to the right of Point M?

  F ⁻6

  G ⁻4

  H ⁻3

  J ⁻1

Oral Directions Choose the correct letter for each answer.

© Scott Foresman

Name two integers that are greater than and two integers that are less than ⁻4.

Name _____

Comparing and Ordering Integers

Example 1

Compare. Use >, <, or = for each ●.

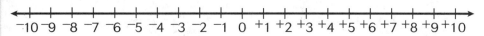

a. ⁻1 ● ⁻3

Since ⁻1 is farther to the
right on the number line,
⁻1 > ⁻3.

b. ⁻2 ● ⁺5

Since ⁻2 is farther to the
left on the number line,
⁻2 < ⁺5 or ⁺5 > ⁻2.

Example 2

Use the number line above to order ⁺3, ⁻2, 0, ⁺6, and ⁻8 from least to greatest.

To order integers, you can first locate them on the number line.
Then write the numbers from left to right.

From least to greatest, the integers are ⁻8, ⁻2, 0, ⁺3, ⁺6.

Compare. Use >, <, or = for each ●.

1 ⁻5 ● ⁻1

2 ⁺3 ● ⁻4

3 ⁻1 ● ⁺7

4 ⁺6 ● ⁻6

5 ⁻2 ● 0

6 ⁻4 ● ⁻9

Order from least to greatest.

7 ⁺2, ⁻5, ⁺6, ⁻4

_____

8 ⁻7, ⁻8, ⁺7, ⁺8

_____

9 0, ⁻3, ⁻4, ⁺1

_____

10 ⁺9, ⁺4, ⁻5, ⁻1

_____

11 ⁻4, ⁻6, 0, ⁺6

_____

12 ⁻6, ⁻1, ⁻4, ⁻7

_____

Name _____

Comparing and Ordering Integers (continued)

Compare. Use >, <, or = for each ●.

13 ⁻2 ● ⁻3   **14** ⁻1 ● ⁺1   **15** 0 ● ⁺5

16 ⁻4 ● ⁻2   **17** ⁻6 ● ⁻7   **18** ⁻5 ● ⁻6

Order from least to greatest.

19 ⁺2, ⁻3, ⁻1, ⁻7   **20** 0, ⁻5, ⁻9, ⁺5   **21** ⁻4, ⁻3, ⁺1, ⁺6

_____   _____   _____

22 ⁺3, ⁻1, ⁺7, ⁺4   **23** ⁻5, 0, ⁻1, ⁻8   **24** ⁻2, ⁺4, ⁻3, ⁻6

_____   _____   _____

25 A hiker started at an elevation of ⁻100 feet and ended at an elevation of ⁻50 feet. Did the hiker move up or down in elevation?   _____

26 **Algebra** If ⁻3 < n, which negative integers could n equal?   _____

27 **Math Reasoning** Name two positive and two negative integers that are greater than ⁻5.

_____

28 **Test Prep** Choose the correct letter for each answer.

Which of these integers is less than ⁻8?

A ⁻5   **B** ⁺4   **C** 0   **D** ⁻10

29 Which of the following temperatures is lower than a temperature of ⁻6°?

F ⁻5°F   **G** ⁻78°F   **H** ⁻4°F   **J** 0°F

Name _____

Comparing and Ordering Integers

1 Which of these integers is greater than ⁻4?

A ⁻3

B ⁻5

C 0

D Both A and C

2 Which of these integers is less than ⁻7?

F ⁻2

G 0

H ⁺3

J ⁻8

3 Which of the following is the correct ordering of ⁺7, ⁻3, 0, ⁻4, ⁺1 from least to greatest?

A ⁻3, ⁻4, 0, ⁺1, ⁺7

B ⁻4, ⁻3, 0, ⁺1, ⁺7

C 0, ⁺1, ⁻3, ⁻4, ⁺7

D ⁻3, ⁻4, ⁺1, ⁺7, 0

4 Which of the following is the correct ordering of ⁻1, ⁻9, ⁻3, ⁻7, ⁻2 from least to greatest?

F ⁻9, ⁻7, ⁻3, ⁻2, ⁻1

G ⁻1, ⁻2, ⁻3, ⁻7, ⁻9

H ⁻9, ⁻7, ⁻1, ⁻2, ⁻3

J ⁻1, ⁻2, ⁻9, ⁻7, ⁻3

5 Which of these elevations is higher than an elevation of ⁻28 feet?

A ⁻30 feet

B ⁻40 feet

C ⁻20 feet

D ⁻38 feet

6 Which of these temperatures is lower than a temperature of ⁻10°F?

F ⁻2°F

G ⁺5°F

H 0°F

J ⁻12°F

Oral Directions Choose the correct letter for each answer.

Can the sum of two negative integers ever equal a positive number? Explain.

Adding Integers

Example

Find $^+5$ + $^-8$.

To find $^+5$ + $^-8$, think of walking on a number line. Use the following rule:
Walk forward for positive numbers, backward for negative numbers.

Start at 0 facing the positive numbers.   Then walk backward
Walk forward 5 steps for $^+5$.   8 steps for $^-8$

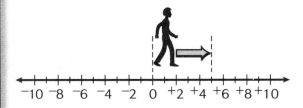   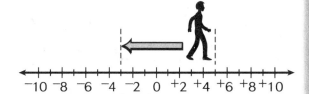

So, $^+5$ + $^-8$ = $^-3$.

Add. Use a number line.

1 $^-4$ + $^-1$ _____   **2** $^+3$ + $^-2$ _____   **3** $^-6$ + $^+7$ _____

4 $^+13$ + $^-5$ _____   **5** $^-1$ + $^-8$ _____   **6** $^-10$ + $^-3$ _____

7 $^-9$ + $^+4$ _____   **8** $^-4$ + $^-7$ _____   **9** $^+6$ + $^-8$ _____

10 $^+5$ + $^+7$ _____   **11** $^+11$ + $^-9$ _____ **12** $^-13$ + $^-1$ _____

13 $^-9$ + $^+6$ _____   **14** $^-6$ + $^+8$ _____   **15** $^-2$ + $^-5$ _____

16 $^-13$ + $^-2$ _____ **17** $^-15$ + $^+3$ _____ **18** $^+6$ + $^-11$ _____

19 $^+10$ + $^-3$ _____ **20** $^-8$ + $^-7$ _____   **21** $^+9$ + $^-7$ _____

Adding Integers (continued)

Add. Use a number line.

22 $^-18 + ^-2$ _____ **23** $^-5 + ^+7$ _____ **24** $^-3 + ^-4$ _____

25 $^-6 + ^+6$ _____ **26** $^+12 + ^-3$ _____ **27** $^+7 + ^-12$ _____

28 $^-2 + ^-8$ _____ **29** $^+5 + ^-18$ _____ **30** $^-1 + ^-11$ _____

31 $^+10 + ^-15$ _____ **32** $^-6 + ^-9$ _____ **33** $^+8 + ^-3$ _____

34 Brent was standing in a valley at an elevation of $^-30$ feet. He decided to walk uphill to increase his elevation by 50 feet. What was his elevation? _____

35 **Mental Math** What is the sum of $^+100$, $^-100$, $^+30$, $^-50$, and $^+50$?

_____

36 **Algebra** Solve $^-3 + n = ^-5$.

_____

37 **Math Reasoning** If the sum of two numbers is a negative number, what can you say about the numbers?

_____

38 **Test Prep** Choose the correct letter for each answer.

What is the sum of $^-14$ and $^+7$?

A $^+7$ **B** $^-7$ **C** $^+2$ **D** 0 **E** NH

39 The temperature at 6:00 A.M. was $^-5°F$. By 10.00 A.M. the temperature had increased by 8 degrees. What was the temperature at 10:00 A.M.?

F $^+13°F$ **G** $^-13°F$ **H** $^+3°F$ **J** $^-3°F$ **K** NH

Name _____

Adding Integers

1 Find ⁻6 + ⁻3.

   A ⁻18

   B ⁻9

   C ⁻9

   D ⁻12

2 What is the sum of ⁻15 and ⁺25?

   F ⁺40

   G ⁻10

   H ⁻40

   J ⁺10

3 Which of these statements is true?

   A The sum of two integers is always negative.

   B If the sum of two negative integers is positive, then both numbers are positive.

   C The sum of two negative integers is negative.

   D If the sum of two integers is negative, then both numbers are positive.

4 What is the sum of ⁺16 and ⁻3?

   F ⁺13

   G ⁻13

   H ⁺19

   J ⁻19

5 The temperature was ⁺5°F at 6:00 P.M. It had dropped 10 degrees by midnight. What was the temperature at midnight?

   A ⁺15°F

   B ⁺5°F

   C ⁺10°F

   D ⁻5°F

6 Which of the following addition problems does NOT give a result of ⁻3?

   F ⁻6 + ⁺3

   G ⁺6 + ⁻9

   H ⁺15 + ⁻12

   J ⁻20 + ⁺17

Oral Directions Choose the correct letter for each answer.

Find two integers whose sum is $^-1$, and whose difference is $^-5$ or $^+5$, depending on the order of the numbers.

Subtracting Integers

Example 1

Find $^-2 - {}^+6$.

Start at zero. Walk backward 2 steps for $^-2$.

The subtraction sign, $-$, means turn around

Then walk forward 6 steps for $^+6$.

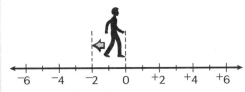

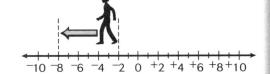

You stop at $^-8$, so $^-2 - {}^+6 = {}^-8$.

Example 2

Find $^-5 - {}^-7$.

To subtract an integer, add the opposite.

$^-5 - {}^-7 = {}^-5 + {}^+7 = {}^+2$

Rewrite each subtraction problem using addition.

1 $^-1 - {}^-8$ _____

2 $^+3 - {}^-4$ _____

3 $^-8 - {}^+2$ _____

4 $^+6 - {}^+3$ _____

5 $^-10 - {}^-7$ _____

6 $^+1 - {}^-4$ _____

Subtract.

7 $^-2 - {}^-5$ _____

8 $^+3 - {}^-8$ _____

9 $^-13 - {}^+6$ _____

10 $^+1 - {}^-6$ _____

11 $^-12 - {}^+5$ _____

12 $^-9 - {}^-3$ _____

13 $^-8 - {}^+4$ _____

14 $^+7 - {}^-3$ _____

15 $^+15 - {}^+9$ _____

Subtracting Integers (continued)

Rewrite each subtraction problem using addition.

16 $^-15 - {}^-1$ _____

17 $^-3 - {}^+8$ _____

18 $^+6 - {}^+7$ _____

19 $^-9 - {}^-4$ _____

20 $^+12 - {}^-1$ _____

21 $^-18 - {}^+6$ _____

Subtract.

22 $^-16 - {}^-1$ _____

23 $^-2 - {}^+5$ _____

24 $^-1 - {}^-9$ _____

25 $^+5 - {}^-6$ _____

26 $^-7 - {}^-3$ _____

27 $^+10 - {}^+11$ _____

28 $^+3 - {}^+12$ _____

29 $^+8 - {}^-10$ _____

30 $^-11 - {}^-7$ _____

31 The coldest temperature ever recorded in North America was $^-81°F$. The coldest temperature ever recorded in South America was $^-27°F$. How much colder is the low temperature for North America than for South America?

_____

32 **Algebra** Solve $n - {}^-5 = {}^+1$.

_____

33 **Algebra** Solve $m - {}^+3 = {}^-2$.

_____

34 **Math Reasoning** If two negative integers are subtracted, is the result always negative? Explain.

_____

35 **Test Prep** Choose the correct letter for the answer.

Find $^-11 - {}^-6$.

A $^-5$ **B** $^-4$ **C** $^+5$ **D** $^+7$ **E** NH

Subtracting Integers

1 Find $^-3 - {}^-5$.

A $^+2$

B $^-2$

C $^-8$

D $^+8$

2 Which of the following integer subtraction problems does NOT give a result of $^+6$?

F $^+9 - {}^+3$

G $^-12 - {}^-6$

H $^+3 - {}^-3$

J $^-14 - {}^-20$

3 Find $^+4 - {}^+12$.

A $^+16$

B $^-16$

C $^+8$

D $^-8$

4 Which of these integer subtraction problems is NOT correct?

F $^-1 - {}^-5 = {}^+4$

G $^+3 - {}^-9 = {}^-6$

H $^-4 - {}^+3 = {}^-7$

J $^+8 - {}^+10 = {}^-2$

5 Joey stood in a valley at an elevation of $^-50$ feet. From there he went down into a cave 30 feet deep. What was his elevation in the bottom of the cave?

A $^-80$ feet

B $^-20$ feet

C $^+80$ feet

D $^+20$ feet

6 The temperature on one cold day was $^-1°F$ and then dropped 5 degrees that night. What was the temperature?

F $^-6°F$

G $^+4°F$

H $^+6°F$

J $^-4°F$

Oral Directions Choose the correct letter for each answer.

Evaluate the expression $^-5 + y$ for all integers from $^-3$ to $^+3$.

Name _____

Evaluating Expressions with Integers

Example 1

Evaluate $x + {}^-6$, when $x = {}^-13$.

$x + {}^-6 = {}^-13 + {}^-6$ Replace x with ${}^-13$.

       $= {}^-19$

Example 2

Evaluate $m - n + p$ for $m = {}^-3$, $n = {}^-1$, and $p = {}^-4$.

$m - n + p = {}^-3 - {}^-1 + {}^-4$ Replace m with ${}^-3$, n with ${}^-1$, and p with ${}^-4$.

          $= {}^-3 + {}^+1 + {}^-4$ Rewrite subtraction as addition of the opposite.

          $= {}^-2 + {}^-4$ Add ${}^-3$ and ${}^+1$.

          $= {}^-6$ Add ${}^-2$ and ${}^-4$.

Evaluate each expression for $x = {}^-10$ and $x = {}^+5$.

1 $x + 6$ **2** $x - 9$ **3** $6 - x$

_____   _____   _____

4 $x - 18$ **5** ${}^-12 + x$ **6** ${}^-2 - x$

_____   _____   _____

7 ${}^-7 + x$ **8** $x + x$ **9** $x - x$

_____   _____   _____

10   Evaluate $a - b - c$ for $a = {}^-2$, $b = {}^-5$, and $c = {}^+6$.   _____

11   Evaluate $p + q - r$ for $p = {}^-7$, $q = {}^+3$, and $r = {}^-4$.   _____

12   Evaluate $x - y + z$ for $x = {}^+10$, $y = {}^-6$, and $z = {}^-5$.   _____

Evaluating Expressions with Integers (continued)

Evaluate each expression for $x = {}^+6$ and $x = {}^-7$.

13 $3 + x$ _____ **14** ${}^-8 - x$ _____

15 $x - 4$ _____ **16** $x + 6$ _____

17 $x - 12$ _____ **18** ${}^-5 + x$ _____

19 Evaluate $d - e - f$ for $d = 28$, $e = 25$, and $f = {}^-4$. _____

20 Evaluate $g + h - j$ for $g = {}^+6$, $h = {}^-10$, and $j = {}^-1$. _____

21 Evaluate $s - t + v$ for $s = {}^-11$, $t = {}^-4$, and $v = {}^+9$. _____

22 **Mental Math** Evaluate $u - v$ for $u = 15$, and $v = 0$. _____

23 **Mental Math** Evaluate $u - v$ for $u = 0$, and $v = {}^-6$. _____

24 **Math Reasoning** When you evaluate $13 + x$ for integer x values, is there any value for x that will make the result zero? If so, what is it? _____

25 **Test Prep** Choose the correct letter for each answer.

Evaluate ${}^-12 - x$ for $x = {}^-4$.

A ${}^-16$ **B** ${}^+16$ **C** ${}^+8$ **D** ${}^-8$ **E** NH

26 Evaluate $s - t - v$ for $s = {}^-2$, $t = {}^-5$, and $v = {}^-7$.

F ${}^-14$ **G** ${}^+10$ **H** 0 **J** ${}^-4$ **K** NH

Name _____

Evaluating Expressions with Integers

1 Evaluate $^-6 - x$ for $x = {}^-9$.

   A $^-3$

   B $^-15$

   C $^+3$

   D $^+15$

2 Evaluate $n - {}^+12$ for $n = {}^-4$.

   F $^-16$

   G $^+16$

   H $^+8$

   J $^-8$

3 Which value of t makes $5 - t$ equal to 0?

   A $t = 0$

   B $t = {}^+5$

   C $t = {}^-5$

   D $t = {}^-4$

4 Evaluate $a + b - c$ for $a = {}^-4$, $b = {}^+5$, and $c = {}^-6$.

   F $^-5$

   G $^-7$

   H $^-5$

   J $^+7$

5 Evaluate $u - v - w$ for $u = {}^-9$, $v = {}^-8$, and $w = {}^+7$.

   A $^-8$

   B $^-10$

   C $^+8$

   D $^+10$

6 Which values of x and y make $x - y$ equal to $^-3$?

   F $x = {}^+5$ and $y = {}^+2$

   G $x = {}^-7$ and $y = {}^+4$

   H $x = {}^-9$ and $y = {}^-6$

   J $x = {}^-1$ and $y = {}^-4$

Oral Directions Choose the correct letter for each answer.

On a coordinate grid, plot these points, connect them, and tell what shape they make:
$(0, 1), (6, 1),$
$(5, {}^-1), ({}^-1, {}^-1).$

Name _____

Example 1

Graph the ordered pair (⁺3, ⁻1).

- Begin at the origin.

- Move right 3 units on the x-axis since ⁺3 is a positive integer.

- Then move down 1 unit since ⁻1 is a negative integer.

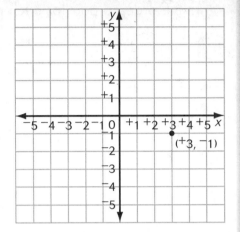

Example 2

Look at the grid at the right.

Name the ordered pair for each point shown.

Point A   (⁺2, ⁻3)

Point B   (⁻1, ⁺4)

Point C   (⁺1, ⁺3)

Point D   (⁻2, ⁻4)

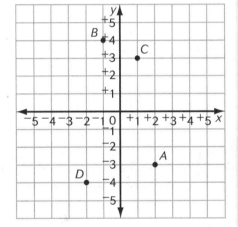

Write the ordered pair for each point.

1 E _____   **2** F _____

3 G _____   **4** H _____

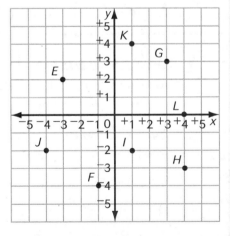

Name the point for each ordered pair.

5 (⁺4, 0) _____   **6** (⁺1, ⁻2) _____

7 (⁺1, ⁺4) _____   **8** (⁻4, ⁻2) _____

Name _____

Graphing Points in the Coordinate Plane (continued)

Write the ordered pair for each point.

9 M _____

10 N _____

11 P _____

12 Q _____

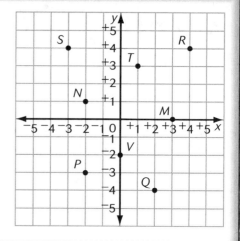

Name the point for each ordered pair.

13 $(^+1, ^+3)$ _____

14 $(^+4, ^+4)$ _____

15 $(0, ^-2)$ _____

16 $(^-3, ^+4)$ _____

17 Which point is located by starting at the origin, moving 3 units left and 4 units down? _____

18 Which point is located by starting at the origin and moving 5 units up? _____

19 **Math Reasoning** What is the y-coordinate for any point on the x-axis? _____

20 **Test Prep** Choose the correct letter for each answer.

What is the ordered pair for A?

A $(^+4, ^+2)$ **C** $(^-2, ^-4)$

B $(^+2, ^+4)$ **D** $(^-4, ^-2)$

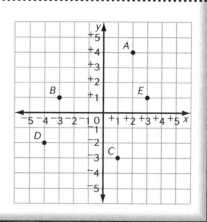

21 Which point is located at $(^-3, 1)$?

F B   **G** C   **H** D   **J** E

Name _____

Use the figure below to answer
Exercises 1–6.

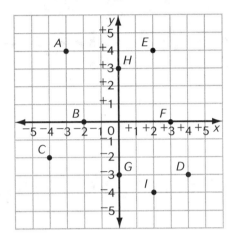

1 What is the ordered pair for *E*?

A (⁻2, ⁻4)

B (⁻4, ⁻2)

C (⁺2, ⁺4)

D (⁺4, ⁺2)

2 What is the ordered pair for *A*?

F (⁻3, ⁺4)

G (⁺3, ⁺4)

H (⁺4, ⁻3)

J (⁺4, ⁺3)

3 Which point is located
at (0, ⁻3)?

A *B*

B *F*

C *H*

D *G*

4 Which point is located
at (2, ⁻4)?

F *C*

G *E*

H *I*

J *B*

5 Which pair of points has an
x-coordinate of 2?

A *E* and *I*

B *G* and *D*

C *H* and *G*

D *A* and *E*

6 Which pair of points
has a *y*-coordinate of 0?

F *G* and *D*

G *B* and *F*

H *H* and *G*

J *A* and *E*

Oral Directions Choose the correct letter for each answer.

Graph the equation $y = x + {}^-2$. Make a table. Use at least 3 values for x. Does the point $({}^-1, {}^-4)$ fall on the line?

Name _____

Example 1

For the equation $y = x - {}^+1$, find y when $x = {}^-2$, when $x = 0$, and when $x = {}^+4$. Name the ordered pairs.

When $x = {}^-2$,

$y = x - {}^+1$

$y = {}^-2 - {}^+1$

$y = {}^-3$

When $x = 0$,

$y = x - {}^+1$

$y = 0 - {}^+1$

$y = {}^-1$

When $x = {}^+4$,

$y = x - {}^+1$

$y = {}^+4 - {}^+1$

$y = {}^+3$

The ordered pairs are $({}^-2, {}^-3)$, $(0, {}^-1)$, and $({}^+4, {}^+3)$.

Example 2

Graph the equation $y = x + {}^+3$.

Make a table.

Substitute any three values for x and find the corresponding y values. Plot the points and connect the points to graph the equation.

x	y
⁻2	⁺1
0	⁺3
⁺1	⁺4

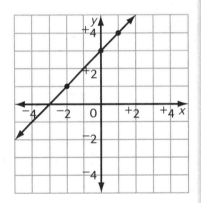

For each equation, find the value of y when $x = {}^-4$, when $x = 0$, and when $x = {}^+2$. Then name the ordered pairs.

1 $y = x - {}^+5$ _____

2 $y = {}^+2 + x$ _____

3 $y = x + {}^+6$ _____

4 $y = {}^+4 - x$ _____

5 $y = x - {}^+3$ _____

Graphing Equations (continued)

Graph each equation. First make a table using x-values of ⁻3, 0, and 3.

6 $y = x + {}^+2$

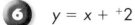

x	y

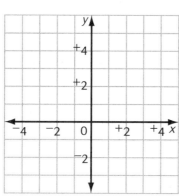

7 $y = 1 - {}^+x$

x	y

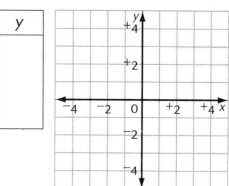

8 $y = x - {}^+3$

x	y

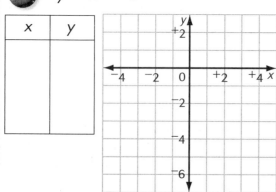

9 $y = {}^+2 - x$

x	y

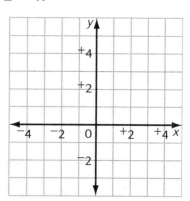

10 **Math Reasoning** Is the point (⁺6, ⁻1) on the graph of $y = {}^+5 - x$? Explain.

_____

_____

11 **Test Prep** Choose the correct letter for the answer.

Which of the following is a correct table for $y = x - {}^+4$?

A

x	y
⁻2	⁻4
0	⁻2
⁺2	0

B

x	y
⁻2	⁻3
0	⁻1
⁺2	⁺1

C

x	y
⁻2	⁺2
0	⁺4
⁺2	⁺6

D

x	y
⁻2	⁻6
0	⁻4
⁺2	⁻2

Name _____

1 Which ordered pair represents the equation $y = {}^+3 - x$ when $x = {}^-1$?

    A $({}^-1, {}^+2)$ **C** $({}^+4, {}^-1)$

    B $({}^+2, {}^+1)$ **D** $({}^-1, {}^+4)$

2 Which of the following is a correct table for $y = x + {}^+5$?

F

x	y
⁻1	⁻4
0	⁺5
⁺1	⁺6

H

x	y
⁻1	⁺6
0	⁺5
⁺1	⁺4

G

x	y
⁻1	⁺4
0	⁺5
⁺1	⁺6

J

x	y
⁻1	⁺0
0	⁺1
⁺1	⁺2

3 Which y value represents the equation $y = x - {}^+6$ when $x = {}^-5$?

    A $^+11$ **C** $^-11$

    B $^-1$ **D** $^+1$

4 Which of the graphs to the right is the correct graph for the equation $y = {}^+2 + x$?

Oral Directions Choose the correct letter for each answer.

F
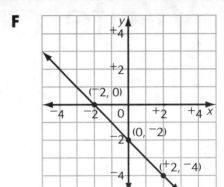

G
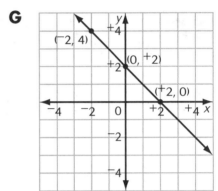

H
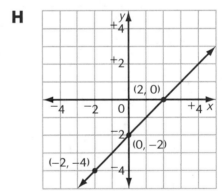

J
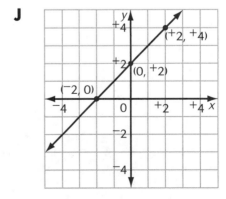

Write an equation to show the relationship between x and y. Use the equation to find y when $x = 7$.

x	1	2	3	4
y	3	4	5	6

Writing Equations

Example 1

Examine the values in the table at the right and write an equation that describes the relationship between x and y.

Notice that each y-value is always 1 less than the corresponding x-value. The relationship can be described by the equation $y = x - {}^+1$.

x	y
$^-2$	$^-3$
$^-1$	$^-2$
0	$^-1$
$^+1$	0
$^+2$	$^+1$

Example 2

Look at the graph of the line at the right. Find the equation that describes the relationship between x and y.

Make a table and look for a pattern that can help you describe the relationship between x and y.

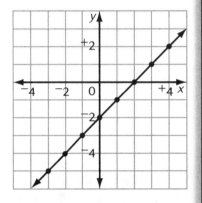

x	$^-3$	$^-2$	$^-1$	0	$^+1$	$^+2$	$^+3$	$^+4$
y	$^-5$	$^-4$	$^-3$	$^-2$	$^-1$	0	$^+1$	$^+2$

Each y-value is 2 less than the x-value.
The equation of the line is $y = x - {}^+2$.

. . . .

Write an equation that describes the relationship between x and y.

1

x	y
$^-2$	$^+4$
$^-1$	$^+5$
0	$^+6$
$^+1$	$^+7$
$^+2$	$^+8$

_____

2

x	y
$^-2$	$^-6$
$^-1$	$^-5$
0	$^-4$
$^+1$	$^-3$
$^+2$	$^-2$

_____

3

x	y
$^-2$	$^-9$
$^-1$	$^-8$
0	$^-7$
$^+1$	$^-6$
$^+2$	$^-5$

_____

4

x	y
$^-2$	$^+6$
$^-1$	$^+7$
0	$^+8$
$^+1$	$^+9$
$^+2$	$^+10$

_____

Writing Equations (continued)

Write an equation that describes the relationship between x and y.

5

x	y
⁻2	⁻7
⁻1	⁻6
0	⁻5
⁺1	⁻4
⁺2	⁻3

_____

6

x	y
⁻2	⁻1
⁻1	0
0	⁺1
⁺1	⁺2
⁺2	⁺3

_____

7

x	y
⁻2	⁻11
⁻1	⁻10
0	⁻9
⁺1	⁻8
⁺2	⁻7

_____

8

x	y
⁻2	⁻5
⁻1	⁻4
0	⁻3
⁺1	⁻2
⁺2	⁻1

9 Make a table of values to describe the graph. Then write an equation.

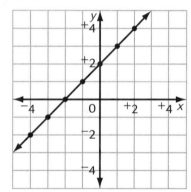

x						
y						

_____

10 **Test Prep** Choose the correct letter for the answer.

Which equation describes the graph at the right?

A $y = x - {}^{+}4$

B $y = x + {}^{+}3$

C $y = x + {}^{+}5$

D $y = x + {}^{+}1$

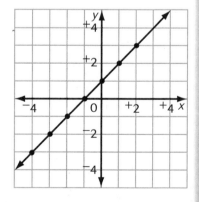

Name _____

1 Which equation describes the relationship between x and y in the table below?

x	⁻2	⁻1	0	⁺1	⁺2
y	⁺3	⁺4	⁺5	⁺6	⁺7

A $y = x - {}^+5$

B $y = x + {}^+3$

C $y = x + {}^+2$

D $y = x + {}^+5$

2 Which equation describes the graph below?

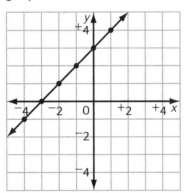

F $y = x - {}^+3$

G $y = x + {}^+3$

H $y = x + {}^+2$

J $y = x - {}^+2$

3 Which table describes the graph below?

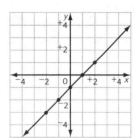

A
x	⁻2	⁻1	0	⁺1	⁺2
y	⁻3	⁻2	⁻1	0	⁺1

B
x	⁻2	⁻1	0	⁺1	⁺2
y	⁻2	⁻1	0	⁺1	⁺2

C
x	⁻2	⁻1	0	⁺1	⁺2
y	⁻1	0	⁺1	⁺2	⁺3

D
x	⁻3	⁻2	⁻1	0	⁺1
y	⁻2	⁻1	0	⁺1	⁺2

4 Which equation describes the relationship between x and y in the table below?

x	⁻2	⁻1	0	⁺1	⁺2
y	⁺6	⁺7	⁺8	⁺9	⁺10

F $y = x + {}^+4$

G $y = x + {}^+6$

H $y = x + {}^+8$

J $y = x - {}^+9$

Oral Directions Choose the correct letter for each answer.

Tools Contents

10 × 10 Chart
